ANTEPOST

Published in Milano (Italy) 2026

ISBN 979-1282522014

ANTEPOST
Cover art: portrait of ***Antonia Pozzi***, mixed media with oil on paper, ***Francesca Draetta,*** **2025** (private property)

ANTONIA POZZI

Translated by Stefania Lucchetti

Portrait of Antonia Pozzi – Francesca Draetta © 2025

Contents

Antonia Pozzi: A Biographical Introduction

Antonia Pozzi (1912–1938) occupies a singular and haunting place in twentieth-century Italian literature. Although none of her poems were published during her lifetime, her work has since come to be recognized as one of the most intimate and original lyric voices of her generation. Her writing, discovered only after her early death, reveals a sensibility poised between the worlds she inhabited: the cultivated, bourgeois Milan of her upbringing, and the wild mountain landscapes the Valsassina, where she sought freedom, clarity, and refuge. To approach Pozzi is to encounter a life lived in acute perception, in emotional intensity, and in the intimacy of a talent that matured almost secretly.

Antonia Pozzi was born in Milan on February 13, 1912, into a cultivated and socially prominent family. Her father, Roberto Pozzi, was a respected lawyer; her mother, Countess Carolina Cavagna Sangiuliani di Gualdana, belonged to an aristocratic lineage distinguished by artistic and intellectual traditions. Pozzi grew up in an environment shaped by literature, music, foreign languages, and the visual arts: an upbringing that fostered her early literary vocation. She had a tender and deep affection for her grandmother Maria (whom she called Nena).

From childhood, Pozzi spent long periods in Pasturo, a village in the Valsassina valley at the foot of the Grigna mountains, where her family owned a second home. The alpine landscape of the Lombardy region - its rock faces, snowfields, meadows, and silence - played a central role in her inner life and creative imagination.

She received a classical education at the Liceo Manzoni in Milan and later enrolled at the University of Milan, where she studied literature and modern philology where she majored under the philosopher Antonio Banfi. Banfi's rationalist and anti-rhetorical approach to culture influenced her deeply, reinforcing her commitment to clarity, ethical seriousness, and stylistic restraint. During her university years, Pozzi formed friendships with several figures who would later become prominent in Italian intellectual life, including Vittorio Sereni, Luciano Anceschi, and Enzo Paci, though she remained largely independent of literary groups or movements. She travelled abroad during holidays and spent time in Great Britain, Austria and Germany studying English and German. She then started teaching in a secondary school in Milano.

Alongside poetry, Pozzi cultivated photography with notable rigor; her photographs reveal a disciplined eye attentive to structure, light, and emotional stillness.

Between her adolescence and early adulthood, Pozzi wrote several hundred poems, as well as diaries and an extensive correspondence. None of her poems were published during her lifetime. Her decision not to seek publication appears to have been deliberate, reflecting both personal reserve and a demanding conception of poetic truth.

In the last decade of her short life, Pozzi experienced increasing emotional distress, compounded by family pressures. Her love story with Antonio Maria Cervi (who had been her former Latin and Greek teacher at Liceo Manzoni in Milan) ended painfully in 1930 as her family intervened and forbade the relationship – which was reputed a scandal not only of age and authority, but also of social reputation. Although she had a second love, she never found the devotion of Cervi's love again.

Her devotion to poetry was questioned by her intellectual circle. She grew an increasing sense of estrangement from the social and cultural world around her.

Although she appeared to live an ordinary life for a young woman of her time, she was consumed by an inner, existential drama that never found peace.

On December 2, 1938, she attempted suicide near the Cistercian abbey of Chiaravalle, on the outskirts of Milan. She died the following day, at the age of twenty-six. Her death was publicly attributed to pneumonia; the true circumstances became known only later.

After her death, her father prepared a private edition of her poems, *Parole* (1939), substantially altering and censoring the manuscripts. Beginning in the 1980s, thanks to the work of scholars and editors such as Onorina Dino and Alessandra Cenni, Pozzi's original texts were restored. Today she is recognized as one of the most distinctive and uncompromising lyric voices of twentieth-century Italian poetry.

TRANSLATOR - Stefania Lucchetti

www.stefanialucchetti.it

Stefania Lucchetti is a bilingual Italian essayist and award-winning poet. She has authored poetry collections and philosophy books on technological humanism. Lucchetti is bilingual (Italian-English) and writes in both languages.
Born in 1975 in Verona, Italy, she saw her first poetry published at 13 while living in the US with her family, marking the beginning of a long journey as wordsmith. She studied classics at Liceo Classico in Gorizia and then went on to obtain a JD in law from Università Cattolica del Sacro Cuore in Milan in 1999, with a thesis on the liberalisation of the telecommunications sector. Among the first Italian lawyers to specialize in telecommunications and new technologies, Lucchetti advised several early internet pioneers during the dot-com boom. She was also the first Italian lawyer to qualify as a solicitor in Hong Kong, after qualifying also in the UK. To enrich her knowledge and writing depth, she also obtained a second master's degree in clinical psychology.
Her bibliographical profile is listed in the archives of Italian Poetry Org, Wikipoesia and Poetesse Donne.

Lucchetti writes a well-loved blog and newsletter on Substack called ESPRESSO VERSES (available both in Italian version and English version) which readers can sign up to from her website https://stefanialucchetti.it/en/
Instagram: @stefania.lucchetti

Portrait of Stefania Lucchetti – Francesca Draetta © 2026

Books by Stefania Lucchetti

Poetry:

- The Adventurous Way Home: Poems of Soul and Hope (Antepost, 2026)
- Love Poems (Antepost, 2026)
- Coffee Stains On My Books (Alchemia, 2024)
- Afternoons of Suspended Love (Alchemia, 2024)
- Penelope's Web (Alchemia, 2024)

Essays:

- The Bricks of the New Babel: Identity, Ethics and Language of Digital Citizenship (Antepost, 2026)
- Ideas in Reality: The Art and Discipline of Thinking and Doing (2nd edition, Alchemia, 2026)
- Virtual Teams (Alchemia, 2023)
- Women Breaking Through Leadership (Hong Kong, 2012)
- (Hong Kong, 2011)
- The Principle of Relevance: The Essential Strategy to Navigate Through the Information Age (Hong Kong, 2010)

Poetry in Translation:

- Antonia Pozzi: Translated by Stefania Lucchetti (Antepost, 2026)
- Ada Negri: Translated by Stefania Lucchetti (Antepost, 2026)
- Poets of the Italian Renaissance: Gaspara Stampa, Veronica Gàmbara, Vittoria Colonna: Translated by Stefania Lucchetti (Antepost, 2026)

A Short Commentary on the Poetry of Antonia Pozzi

by Stefania Lucchetti

To read Antonia Pozzi is to enter the luminous borderlands between yearning and renunciation, between the visible world and the emotional undercurrent beneath it. Her brief life left behind a body of work that feels both intimate and inexhaustible. She wrote privately, almost secretly, yet with an exactness that seems intended for the future. Her poems endure because they contain a rare concentration of truth: a voice that does not ask to be admired, only heard and held.

"Desiderare di donarsi non può non essere la suprema delle aspirazioni di una creatura; ma volersi ad ogni costo donare quando del rifiuto delle cose si ha già coscienza, è uno sconfinato illecito, un proiettarsi in gigantesche fantasie che non hanno più realtà di un'ombra nera sul muro".

Pozzi's poetry inhabits two gravitational fields: the intimacy of the inner life and the immensity of the natural world. In poem after poem, mountains, lakes, wind, reeds, stars, and snow are not metaphors but presences: elders, guardians, mirrors, and sometimes adversaries. The natural world is not outside her; it is the language through which she attempts to understand herself. Landscape becomes a form of thinking, a moral and emotional terrain in which the self measures its own limits.

A defining feature of Pozzi's writing is its emotional honesty. Her poems do not hide the fragility of the self; they protect nothing. The speaker confesses, trembles, offers herself without ornament or defense. This vulnerability is never theatrical. It is lucid, disciplined, and exacting: so articulate that it becomes a form of strength. There is no distancing, no attempt to explain emotion from the outside: only the steady, clear line of lived experience.

For Pozzi, love is both anchor and abyss. It is approached with reverence and fear, often sensed as a force that carries within it the seeds of dissolution. Longing, loss, and the desire for purity recur throughout her work, never sentimentalized, never resolved. Love sharpens perception even as it exposes the self to fracture; it is a site of illumination and risk.

Perhaps what makes Pozzi so compelling to contemporary readers is her ability to articulate a solitude that feels not dated but startlingly modern. Hers is an existential solitude rather than a romantic one, shaped by the distance between the self and the world, between the self and God, and sometimes between the self and poetry itself. In the poems addressed directly to poetry – among her most haunting texts –the speaker asks the art she depends on whether she is still worthy of its presence.

Antonia Pozzi's poetry occupies a rare space where intimacy and vastness coexist. Her work often begins in the immediate: the curve of a shoulder, the trembling of reeds, the weight of an unshed tear. And yet it opens into landscapes of extraordinary depth. Though written in the early decades of the twentieth century, her poems feel startlingly contemporary in their clarity and restraint.

Living in Milan, and walking often through the same neighbourhood where Pozzi herself once lived, I encounter her presence not as a distant literary figure but as a shadow in the city's texture. Her house stands only a short walk from my own. This physical proximity has accompanied my translation work like an undercurrent: a reminder that her poetry emerged not only from mountain solitude but from the life lived in this very city.

In selecting the poems for this collection, I gravitated toward those in which Antonia Pozzi's voice reveals its most intimate tension between vulnerability and clarity: poems where her emotional experience radiates from her pen. I chose verses which trace the arc of her inner life through its essential motifs: love in its many registers: yearning (*Distacco*, *Amore di lontananza*), sensual self-revelation (*Canto della mia nudità*), the trembling need for connection (*Vertigine*), and the fierce devotion of grief (*Vita*, *Il volto nuovo*). Alongside these, I included poems where nature becomes the grammar of her consciousness, as in *Canto selvaggio*, *Attendamento*, and *Amore dell'acqua*, and others where she confronts the demands of poetry itself as vocation and judgement, such as *Preghiera alla poesia*. Finally, I was drawn to pieces that express her unique blend of fragility and strength: her desire to offer herself with purity and humility (*Lieve offerta*, *Bellezza*), her meditations on identity and loss (*La vita sognata*, *Ricongiungimento*), and her profound metaphysical yearning (*Preghiera*, *Giorno dei morti*).

Together, these poems form a constellation that reflects Pozzi's deepest concerns: the search for connection in love, the search for meaning in the tragedies of life, the dialogue between the self and the natural world, and the continual striving toward a truth that is at once human, spiritual, and poetic.

Translation, for me, is neither an act mere transposition nor of embellishment -but of listening: of allowing the original movement of thought and feeling to find expression in another language without losing its tension. In giving Pozzi's words space in English, I try to honour a voice which, against the odds of time and circumstance, continues to grow clearer.

I have not provided commentaries for the individual poems. As a poet, I deeply feel that poetry, especially poetry as intimate as Pozzi's, asks to be encountered without the weight of explanation. To over-interpret her lines would be to risk dimming their natural luminosity. These poems, in their original Italian and in English, are meant to be felt before they are intellectually understood.

As all poems are presented in their original Italian version with my translation on the side, you will find the Italian version on even pages and the English version on odd pages.

"My chaos lies in this: that everything, for me, is a wound through which my personality would like to gush forth in order to give itself. But to give oneself is an act of life that presupposes a reality existing beyond us; and yet everything that calls to me has reality only through my eyes, and when I try to step outside myself – to dissolve my limits into that reality –I find it before me altered, hostile.".

Diary entry by Antonia Pozzi, 4 February 1935[1]
Translation by Stefania Lucchetti

---

[1] http://www.antoniapozzi.it/

Amore di lontananza

Ricordo che, quand'ero nella casa
della mia mamma, in mezzo alla pianura,
avevo una finestra che guardava
sui prati; in fondo, l'argine boscoso
nascondeva il Ticino e, ancor più in fondo,
c'era una striscia scura di colline.
Io allora non avevo visto il mare
che una sol volta, ma ne conservavo
un'aspra nostalgia da innamorata.
Verso sera fissavo l'orizzonte;
socchiudevo un po' gli occhi; accarezzavo
i contorni e i colori tra le ciglia:
e la striscia dei colli si spianava,
tremula, azzurra: a me pareva il mare
e mi piaceva più del mare vero.

Milano, 24 aprile 1929

Love from afar

I remember that, when I was in the house,
of my mom, out on the plain,
I had a window that looked
over the meadows; farther off, the wooded embankment
hid the Ticino, and farther still
there was a dark strip of hills.
Then I had seen the sea
only once, yet I kept
a harsh nostalgia for it, like one in love.
Toward evening I would stare at the horizon;
I half-closed my eyes; I caressed
shapes and colors through my lashes:
and the strip of hills would flatten out,
tremulous, blue: it seemed the sea to me,
and I liked it more than the real sea.

Milan, 24 April 1929

Riscatti illeciti

Da un pianoforte, dietro la parete,
gocciola qualche nota smorta,
punteggiatura ai nostri pensieri.
Tu mi parli di tua madre morta:
e la mia animetta sbiadita
si stiracchia in singhiozzi,
per riscattare col dolore altrui
la sua inutile vita.

Milano, 25 Aprile 1929

Illicit redemptions

From a piano, behind the wall,
a few dull notes drip,
punctuation to our thoughts.
You speak to me of your dead mother:
and my faded little soul
stretches into sobs,
to redeem with another's pain
its own useless life.

Milano, 25 April 1929

Distacco
a T. F.

Tu, partita.
Senza desiderare la parola
che avevo in cuore e che non seppi dire.
Nel vano della porta, il nostro bacio
(lieve, ché ti eri appena incipriata)
quasi spaccato in due da un gran barbaglio
di luce, che veniva dalle scale.
Io rimasta
lungamente al mio tavolo, dinnanzi
a un vecchio ritrattino della mamma,
specchiando fissamente dentro il vetro
i miei occhi febbrili, inariditi.

Milano, 9 maggio 1929

Parting
to T.F.

You, gone.
Without wanting the word
I had in my heart and were not able to say.
In the doorway, our kiss
(light, since you had just powdered yourself)
almost split in two by a great glare
of light coming up from the stairs.
I remained
for a long while at my table, before
an old little portrait of my mother,
reflecting fixedly into the glass
my own eyes - feverish, dried out.

Milan, 9 May 1929

Lagrime

Bambina, ho visto che stasera hai pianto,
mentre la mamma tua sonava: pochi,
per questo pianto, i tuoi quindici anni.
So che forse noi siamo creature
nate tutte da un'ansia eterna: il mare;
e che la vita, quando fruga e strazia
l'essere nostro, spreme dal profondo
un po' del sale da cui fummo tratte.
Ma non sono per te le salse lagrime.
Lascia ch'io sola pianga, se qualcuno
suona, in un canto, qualche nenia triste.
La musica: una cosa fonda e trepida
come una notte rorida di stelle,
come l'anima sua. Lascia ch'io pianga.
Perch'io non potrò mai avere – intendi? –
né le stelle,
né lui.

Varese – Milano, 11 luglio 1929

Tears

Child, I saw that this evening you cried,
while your mother was playing music: too few,
for such weeping, your fifteen years.
I know that perhaps we are all creatures
born of a single, eternal anxiety: the sea;
and that life, when it rummages and rends
our being, wrings from our depths
a little of the salt from which we were drawn.
But salty tears are not for you.
Let me alone weep, if someone
plays, in a corner, some sad little lullaby.
Music: something deep and trembling
like a night wet with stars,
like her soul. Let me weep.
For I shall never be able to have - do you understand? -
neither the stars,
nor him.

Varese - Milano, 11 July 1929

Canto selvaggio

Ho gridato di gioia, nel tramonto.
Cercavo i ciclamini fra i rovai:
ero salita ai piedi di una roccia
gonfia e rugosa, rotta di cespugli.
Sul prato crivellato di macigni,
sul capo biondo delle margherite,
sui miei capelli, sul mio collo nudo,
dal cielo alto si sfaldava il vento.
Ho gridato di gioia, nel discendere.
Ho adorato la forza irta e selvaggia
che fa le mie ginocchia avide al balzo;
la forza ignota e vergine, che tende
me come un arco nella corsa certa.
Tutta la via sapeva di ciclami;
i prati illanguidivano nell'ombra,
frementi ancora di carezze d'oro.
Lontano, in un triangolo di verde,
il sole s'attardava. Avrei voluto
scattare, in uno slancio, a quella luce;
e sdraiarmi nel sole, e denudarmi,
perché il morente dio s'abbeverasse
del mio sangue. Poi restare, a notte,
stesa nel prato, con le vene vuote:
le stelle – a lapidare imbestialite
la mia carne disseccata, morta.

Pasturo, 17 luglio 1929

Wild song

I cried out with joy, at sunset.
I was searching for cyclamens among the brambles:
I had climbed to the foot of a rock,
swollen and wrinkled, broken with shrubs.
Across the meadow riddled with boulders,
over the blond heads of the daisies,
over my hair, over my naked neck,
from the high sky the wind was breaking apart.
I cried out with joy, as I went down.
I adored the bristling, savage force
that makes my knees eager for the leap;
the unknown, virgin force that draws
me taut like a bow in its sure flight.
All the path was scented with cyclamens;
the meadows languished into shadow,
still quivering with golden caresses.
Far off, in a triangle of green,
the sun lingered. I wished
to spring, in a single surge, toward that light;
and to lie stretched in the sun, and strip myself bare,
so that the dying god might drink deep
of my blood. Then to remain, at night,
outstretched on the grass, with emptied veins:
the stars - to stone, in bestial fury,
my dried flesh, dead.

Pastura, 17 July 1929

Canto della mia nudità

Guardami: sono nuda. Dall'inquieto
languore della mia capigliatura
alla tensione snella del mio piede,
io sono tutta una magrezza acerba
inguainata in un color d'avorio.
Guarda: pallida è la carne mia.
Si direbbe che il sangue non vi scorra.
Rosso non ne traspare. Solo un languido
palpito azzurro sfuma in mezzo al petto.
Vedi come incavato ho il ventre. Incerta
è la curva dei fianchi, ma i ginocchi
e le caviglie e tutte le giunture,
ho scarne e salde come un puro sangue.
Oggi, m'inarcherò nuda, nel nitore
del bagno bianco e m'inarcherò nuda
domani sopra un letto, se qualcuno
mi prenderà. E un giorno nuda, sola,
stesa supina sotto troppa terra,
starò, quando la morte avrà chiamato.

Palermo, 20 luglio 1929

Song of my nakedness

Look at me: I am naked. From the restless
languor of my hair
to the slender tension of my foot,
I am all an unripe thinness
sheathed in a colour of ivory.
Look: pale is my flesh.
One would say no blood runs through it.
No red shows through. Only a languid
blue flutter fades across my chest.
See how hollow my belly is. Uncertain
is the curve of my hips, but my knees
and my ankles and all my joints
are lean and firm like those of a thoroughbred.
Today, I will arch naked, in the clarity
of the white bath, and I will arch naked
tomorrow upon a bed, if someone
will possess me. And one day naked, alone,
lying supine beneath too much earth,
I shall lie, when death has called.

Palermo, 20 July 1929

Fuga
ad A.M.C.

Anima, andiamo. Non ti sgomentare
di tanto freddo, e non guardare il lago,
s'esso ti fa pensare ad una piaga
livida e brulicante. Sì, le nubi
gravano sopra i pini ad incupirli.
Ma noi ci porteremo ove l'intrico
dei rami è tanto folto, che la pioggia
non giunge a inumidire il suolo: lieve,
tamburellando sulla volta scura,
essa accompagnerà il nostro cammino.
E noi calpesteremo il molle strato
d'aghi caduti e le ricciute macchie
di licheni e mirtilli; inciamperemo
nelle radici, disperate membra
brancicanti la terra; strettamente
ci addosseremo ai tronchi, per sostegno;
e fuggiremo. Con la piena forza
della carne e del cuore, fuggiremo:
lungi da questo velenoso mondo
che mi attira e respinge. E tu sarai,
nella pineta, a sera, l'ombra china
che custodisce: ed io per te soltanto,
sopra la dolce strada senza meta,
un'anima aggrappata al proprio amore.

Madonna di Campiglio, 11 agosto 1929

Escape

To A.M.C.

Soul, let us go. Do not be daunted
by so much cold, and do not look at the lake
if it makes you think of a livid, swarming wound.
Yes, the clouds
weigh down upon the pines, darkening them.
But we shall carry ourselves where the tangle
of branches is so dense that the rain
does not reach to dampen the ground: lightly,
drumming on the dark vault,
it will accompany our way.
And we shall tread the soft layer
of fallen needles and the curled patches
of lichen and bilberries; we shall stumble
on the roots, desperate limbs
groping for the earth; closely
we shall press ourselves to the trunks, for support;
and we shall flee. With the full force
of flesh and heart, we shall flee:
far from this poisonous world
that draws me and repels me. And you will be,
in the pinewood, at evening, the bent shadow
that keeps watch; and I, for you alone,
upon the sweet road without destination,
a soul clinging to its own love.

Madonna di Campiglio, 11 agosto 1929

Vertigine

Afferrami alla vita,
uomo. La cengia è stretta.
E l'abisso è un rischio spaventoso
che ci vuole assorbire.
Vedi: la falda erbosa, da cui balza
questo zampillo estatico di rupi,
somiglia a un camposanto sconfinato,
con le sue pietre bianche.
Io mi vorrei tuffare a capofitto
nella fluidità vertiginosa;
vorrei piombare sopra un duro masso
e sradicarlo e stritolarlo, io,
con le mie mani scarne;
strappare gli vorrei, siccome a croce
di cimitero, una parola sola
che mi desse la luce. E poi berrei
a gole gioiose il sangue mio.

Afferrami alla vita,
uomo. Passa la nebbia
e lambe e sperde l'incubo mio folle.
Fra poco la vedremo dipanarsi
sopra le valli: e noi saremo in vetta.

Afferrami alla vita. Oh, come dolci
i tuoi occhi esitanti,
i tuoi occhi di puro vetro azzurro!

Pasturo, 22 agosto 1929

Vertigo

Hold me by the waist,
man. The ledge is narrow.
And the abyss is a terrifying danger
that wants to swallow us.
See: the grassy bank, from which leaps
this ecstatic spray of cliffs,
looks like a boundless graveyard,
with its white stones.
I would like to dive headfirst
into its dizzy fluidity;
I would like to plunge upon a hard boulder
and uproot it and crush it, I,
with my lean hands;
I'd like to tear from it, as from a cemetery
Cross, one single word
that could give me the light. And then I'd drink,
with joyous throat, my own blood.

Hold me by the waist,
man. The fog is passing
and licks at, scatters my mad nightmare.
Soon we will see it unravel
above the valleys: and we will be on the summit.

Hold me by the waist. Oh, how sweet
your hesitant eyes,
your eyes of pure blue glass!

Pasturo, 22 August 1929

Pudore

Se qualcuna delle mie povere parole
ti piace
e tu me lo dici
sia pur solo con gli occhi
io mi spalanco
in un riso beato
ma tremo
come una mamma piccola giovane
che perfino arrossisce
se un passante le dice
che il suo bambino è bello.

1 febbraio 1933

Modesty

If one of my poor words
pleases you
and you tell me so
even only with your eyes
I open wide
in a blessed smile
but I tremble
like a small young mother
who even blushes
if a passerby tells her
that her child is beautiful.

1 February 1933

Vita

(alla memoria di A.C.)

No, non sei morto. L'anima agguantata
m'hai e sgualcita, come un foglio sperso;
racchiuse v'hai le transazioni vili
della mia inconscia vita senza Dio;
un cartoccio ne hai fatto, sodo, greve:
scagliato l'hai dentro l'azzurra vampa
dei tuoi canti, squillati a piena gola;
scagliato l'hai dentro la rossa vampa
del tuo sangue d'eroe. No, non sei morto.
In ogni nuovo fiore che invermigli,
silenzioso nel sole, un camposanto,
vive ed arde il tuo sangue; in ogni lacrima
che, nelle notti insonni e solitarie,
beve con le sue ciglia chi è rimasto,
vive e brucia il tuo pianto; e nel mio cuore,
largo di lontananza, tu divampi:
alla mia fonda e cupa tenerezza,
alla rinuncia mia che si dibatte,
tu dài la luce bianca e rassegnata,
tu dài la rossa luce di battaglia.
Tu mi rinsaldi, tu mi rendi pura:
nel mio amore, la tua morte è Vita.

Pasturo, 21 settembre 1929

Life
(in memory of A.C.)

No, you are not dead. My soul
you seized and crumpled, like a lost sheet of paper;
you enclosed within it the vile transactions
of my reckless life without God;
you made of it a bundle, tight, heavy:
you hurled it into the blue blaze
of your songs, cried out at full throat;
you hurled it into the red blaze
of your hero's blood. No, you are not dead.
In every new flower that reddens,
silent in the sun, a graveyard,
your blood lives and burns; in every tear
that, in the sleepless and solitary nights,
is drunk by the lashes of whoever remains,
your weeping lives and smoulders; and in my heart,
wide with distance, you flare up:
to my deep and shadowed tenderness,
to my struggling renunciation,
you give the white and resigned light,
you give the red light of battle.
You strengthen me, you make me pure again:
in my love, your death is Life.

Pasturo, 21 September 1929

Gioia

Lo splendore del sole
ti abbacinava ieri
dolendo
come la piaga
nelle pupille del cieco.
Ma oggi
lo splendore del sole
non è abbastanza lucente
per la lucentezza tua:
nell'infinito mondo non c'è
che questo tuo splendore
vero.

6 marzo 1932

Joy

The splendour of the sun
dazzled you yesterday,
aching
like a wound
in the pupils of the blind.
But today
the splendour of the sun
is not bright enough
for your brightness:
in the infinite world there is nothing but
this splendour of yours
real.

6 March 1932

Limiti

Tante volte ripenso
alla mia cinghia di scuola
grigia, imbratta,
che tutta me coi miei libri serrava
in un unico nodo
sicuro –
Né c'era allora
questo trascendere ansante
questo sconfinamento senza traccia
questo perdersi
che non è ancora morire –
Tante volte piango, pensando
alla mia cinghia di scuola –

Milano, 16 aprile 1932

Limits

So many times I think back
to my school satchel strap,
grey, smudged,
binding all of me with my books
into one single,
secure knot –
Nor was there then
this panting transcendence,
this borderless crossing without trace,
this losing oneself
which is not yet dying –
So many times I weep, thinking
of my school satchel strap –

Milan, 16 April 1932

Preghiera

Signore, tu lo senti
ch'io non ho voce più
per ridire
il tuo canto segreto.
Signore, tu lo vedi
ch'io non ho occhi più
per i tuoi cieli, per le nuvole tue
consolatrici.

Signore, per tutto il mio pianto,
ridammi una stilla di Te
ch'io riviva.

Perché tu sai, Signore,
che in un tempo lontano
anch'io tenni nel cuore
tutto un lago, un gran lago,
specchio di Te.
Ma tutta l'acqua mi fu bevuta,
o Dio,
ed ora dentro il cuore
ho una caverna vuota,
cieca di Te.

Signore, per tutto il mio pianto,
ridammi una stilla di Te,
ch'io riviva.

20 ottobre 1932

Prayer

Lord, you can hear it:
I have no voice left
to speak again
your secret song.
Lord, you can see it:
I have no eyes left
for your skies, for your clouds
that give comfort.

Lord, for all my weeping,
give me back a single drop of You,
that I may live again.

For you know, Lord,
that in a distant time
I too held in my heart
a whole lake, a great lake,
a mirror of You.
But all that water was drunk from me,
o God,
and now within my heart
there is an empty cavern,
blind of You.

Lord, for all my weeping,
give me back a single drop of You,
that I may live again.

20 October 1932

Giorno dei morti

Dall'anima sfinita i sogni
come fogliame cadono
a lembo a lembo.
E resto come un pioppo nudo
a sopportare
con scarne braccia
tutto il peso dei cieli:
l'invariata piana dell'esistenza
mi gela.

Signore Iddio,
fuori di Te non c'è salvezza,
lo so.

Perché dai morti veniamo,
perché ai morti torniamo
e i morti sono in Te
di là dal gran velo del cielo
e vedono l'oro tuo,
Signore,
il mare eterno
di Te.

E la voce del morti
è la tua voce
bronzea
che travolge l'anima.
Non c'è salvezza,
fuori di Te
Signore.
2 novembre 1932

Day of the dead

From my exhausted soul, dreams
fall like foliage,
strip by strip.
And I remain like a naked poplar
to bear,
with gaunt arms,
the whole weight of the skies:
the unchanging plain of existence
freezes me.

Lord,
outside of You there is no salvation,
I know it.
For from the dead we come,
to the dead we return,
and the dead are in You
beyond the great veil of the sky
and they behold Your gold,
Lord,
the eternal sea
of You.

And the voice of the dead
is Your voice,
brazen,
which overwhelms the soul.

There is no salvation
outside of You,
Lord.
2 November 1932

Unicità

Io credo questo:
che non si può cambiar nome,
cambiar volto
alle creature già nate
nel cuore.

E perciò il nostro bimbo
unico
sarà quello
che noi sognammo
nei mattini di giugno
– ti rammenti? –
Quando calpestavamo
le spighe bionde
per cogliere i papaveri
fiammanti
e tutto il cielo era un rombo
d'ali umane
che cercavano il sole.

Io credo questo:
che saprei squarciarmi
con le mie mani
il grembo
prima di dar la vita
ad un figlio non tuo.

2 febbraio 1933

Uniqueness

I believe this:
that one cannot change the name,
change the face
of creatures already born
in the heart.

And therefore our child,
unique,
will be the one
we dreamed
on June mornings
– do you remember? –
When we trampled
the blond ears of wheat
to gather flaming
poppies,
and all the sky was a thunder
of human wings
seeking the sun.

I believe this:
that I would know how to tear open,
with my own hands,
my womb
before giving life
to a child not yours.

2 February 1933

La voce

Aveva voce in te
l'universo
delle cose mute,
la speranza
che sta senz'ali nei nidi,
che sta sotterra
non fiorita.

Aveva voce in te
il mistero
di tutto che presso una morte
vuol diventare vita,
il filo d'erba
sotto le putride foglie,
il primo riso del bimbo salvato
a fianco di un'agonia
in una corsia
d'ospedale.

Or quando cade dagli alti
rami notturni
dei campanili – un rintocco –
e in cuore affonda come
il frutto dentro il campo arato –

allora hai voce
tu in me –
con quella nota
ampia e sola
che dice i sogni sepolti

del mondo, l'oppressa
nostalgia della luce.

10 dicembre 1933

The voice

It had a voice in you
the universe
of mute things,
hope
that stays wingless in nests,
that stays underground,
unflowered.

It had a voice in you
the mystery
of all that, close to a death,
wants to become life:
the blade of grass
beneath the putrid leaves,
the first smile of the saved child
beside an agony
in a hospital
ward.

Now when, from the high
nocturnal branches
of bell towers, falls – a toll –
and sinks into the heart like
fruit into a ploughed field –

then you have a voice
in me –
with that note,
broad and solitary,
that speaks the buried dreams

of the world, the oppressed
longing for light.

10 December 1933

Sterilità

Oh, non volere ch'io torni
per la mia vita
a penare:
non lo sai che sarebbe
come voler seminare
del grano in un cimitero?

E chi vuoi tu che ne mangi
domani
di un tal pane?

Nemmeno un bimbo affamato,
credimi,
nemmeno un cane
percosso.

Perché non c'è vivo
che la sua vita non senta
avvelenata
dall'odore della morte.
Oh, lascia
che solo le smorte
erbe
coronino le tombe –
lascia
che solo qualche inodora margherita
imbianchi
il deserto viale –

Oh, non voler seminare

il grano
in questa mia vita!

24 gennaio 1933

Sterility

Oh, do not wish that I return
for my life
to suffer:
do you not know it would be
like trying to sow
grain in a cemetery?

And who do you think would eat,
tomorrow,
of such bread?

Not even a starving child,
believe me,
not even a beaten
dog.

For there is no living being
who does not feel their life
poisoned
by the smell of death.
Oh, let
only the pallid
weeds
crown the tombs –
let
only a few scentless daisies
whiten
the deserted avenue –

Oh, do not wish to sow

grain
in this life of mine!

24 January 1933

Il volto nuovo

Che un giorno io avessi
un riso
di primavera – è certo;
e non soltanto lo vedevi tu, lo specchiavi
nella tua gioia:
anch'io, senza vederlo, sentivo
quel riso mio
come un lume caldo
sul volto.

Poi fu la notte
e mi toccò esser fuori
nella bufera:
il lume del mio riso
morì.

Mi trovò l'alba
come una lampada spenta:
stupirono le cose
scoprendo
in mezzo a loro
il mio volto freddato.

Mi vollero donare
un volto nuovo.

Come davanti a un quadro di chiesa
che è stato mutato
nessuna vecchia più vuole
inginocchiarsi a pregare

perché non ravvisa le care
sembianze della Madonna
e questa le pare
quasi una donna
perduta –

così oggi il mio cuore
davanti alla mia maschera
sconosciuta.

20 agosto 1933

The new face

That one day I had
a smile
of spring – it is certain;
and not only did you see it, you reflected it
in your joy:
I too, without seeing it, felt
that smile of mine
like a warm light
upon my face.

Then night came,
and I had to be out
in the storm:
the light of my smile
died.

Dawn found me
like an extinguished lamp:
things were astonished,
discovering
among them
my chilled face.

They wished to give me
a new face.

As before a church painting
that has been altered
no old woman any longer wishes
to kneel and pray,

because she no longer recognizes
the dear features of the Madonna
and she seems to her
almost a woman
lost –

so today my heart stands
before my mask,
unknown.

20 August 1933

Attendamento

Stanotte calerà il vento
immenso falco
sulla nostra tenda;
rapirà le nuvole
lacerate.
Sul nostro sonno
le stelle
sciolte dai veli
intrecceranno ghirlande
di fiamma e lentissime danze.
All'alba
sarà tepido il risveglio,
dolce come l'accendersi
di una lampada fioca:
il canto del torrente
sosterrà
fedele
sopra il suo grembo
il silenzio fanciullo.
Per noi, portati
dagli artigli notturni
del vento,
giaceranno i messaggi delle vette
alla soglia:
leggerli sarà lavare
nel puro azzurro
gli occhi le mani
il cuore –

(Breil, luglio 1933) – Pasturo, 21 agosto 1933

Awaiting

Tonight the wind will descend,
an immense falcon,
upon our tent;
it will carry off the
torn clouds.
Over our sleep
the stars,
loosened from their veils,
will weave garlands
of flame and very slow dances.
At dawn
our waking will be mild,
sweet as the lighting
of a dim lamp:
the song of the stream
will hold up,
faithful,
in its lap,
the childlike silence.
For us, carried
by the nocturnal talons
of the wind,
the messages of the peaks
will lie at the threshold:
to read them will be to wash
in the pure blue
the eyes, the hands,
the heart –

(Breil, luglio 1933) – Pasturo, 21 August 1933

Amore dell'acqua

Dalla valle ch'è un lago
di sole – agitato dall'onda
delle campane –
fugge l'ombra
e si aduna
sotto un albero solo
dove il torrente
cade –

Tutta l'ombra e la frescura del mondo
si serrano intorno
alla fronte accaldata
del bimbo
che – sporto sul ciglio –
l'anima abbandonata
svincolare non sa
dalle argentee braccia
della cascata –

12 settembre 1933

Love of water

From the valley that is a lake
of sun – stirred by the wave
of the bells –
the shadow flees
and gathers
beneath a solitary tree
where the stream
falls –

All the shadow and coolness of the world
draw tight around
the heated brow
of the child
who – leaning over the brink –
cannot loosen
his abandoned soul
from the silvery arms
of the waterfall –

12 September 1933

Ricongiungimento

Se io capissi
quel che vuole dire
– non vederti più –
credo che la mia vita
qui – finirebbe.

Ma per me la terra
è soltanto la zolla che calpesto
e l'altra
che calpesti tu:
il resto
è aria
in cui – zattere sciolte – navighiamo
a incontrarci.

Nel cielo limpido infatti
sorgono a volte piccole nubi
fili di lana
o piume – distanti –
e chi guarda di lì a pochi istanti
vede una nuvola sola
che si allontana.

17 settembre 1933

Rejoining

If I understood
what it means
– to never see you again –
I think my life
here – would end.

But to me the earth
is only the clod I tread
and the other
you tread:
the rest
is air
in which – loosened rafts – we sail
to meet one another.

In the clear sky indeed
there sometimes rise small clouds
threads of wool
or feathers – distant –
and whoever looks a few moments later
sees a single cloud
drifting away.

17 September 1933

La vita sognata

Chi mi parla non sa
che io ho vissuto un'altra vita –
come chi dica
una fiaba
o una parabola santa.

Perché tu eri
la purità mia,
tu cui un'onda bianca
di tristezza cadeva sul volto
se ti chiamavo con labbra impure,
tu cui lacrime dolci
correvano nel profondo degli occhi
se guardavamo in alto –
e così ti parevo più bella.

O velo
tu – della mia giovinezza,
mia veste chiara,
verità svanita –
o nodo
lucente – di tutta una vita
che fu sognata – forse –

oh, per averti sognata,
mia vita cara,
benedico i giorni che restano –

il ramo morto di tutti i giorni che restano,
che servono
per piangere te.

25 settembre 1933

The dreamed life

Those who speak to me do not know
that I have lived another life –
as one might say
a fable
or a holy parable.

For you were
my purity,
you upon whose face
a white wave of sadness fell
if I called you with impure lips;
you whose sweet tears
ran in the depths of your eyes
when we looked upward –
and so I seemed lovelier to you.

Oh veil
you – of my youth,
my clear garment,
truth vanished –
Oh shining
knot – of an entire life
that was dreamed – perhaps –

oh, for having dreamed you,
my dear life,
I bless the days that remain –

the dead branch of all the days that remain,
which serve
to weep for you.

25 September 1933

Mattino

A lungo dalla luna infranto
or ricompone il lago
la sua incolumità
cerulea.
Presso l'isola inferma un cipresso
trae dalle nebbie le bende
per le ferite nascoste:
tacito prega, votando
il nuovo giorno – al cielo.

1 ottobre 1933

Morning

Long broken by the moon,
now the lake restores
its cerulean
wholeness.
Near the ailing island a cypress
draws from the mists the bandages
for the hidden wounds:
silent it prays, offering
the new day – to the sky.

1 October 1933

Bellezza

Ti do me stessa,
le mie notti insonni,
i lunghi sorsi
di cielo e stelle – bevuti
sulle montagne,
la brezza dei mari percorsi
verso albe remote.

Ti do me stessa,
il sole vergine dei miei mattini
su favolose rive
tra superstiti colonne
e ulivi e spighe.

Ti do me stessa,
i meriggi
sul ciglio delle cascate,
i tramonti
ai piedi delle statue, sulle colline,
fra tronchi di cipressi animati
di nidi –

E tu accogli la mia meraviglia
di creatura,
il mio tremito di stelo
vivo nel cerchio
degli orizzonti,
piegato al vento
limpido – della bellezza:
e tu lascia ch'io guardi questi occhi

che Dio ti ha dati,
così densi di cielo –
profondi come secoli di luce
inabissati al di là
delle vette –

4 dicembre 1934

Beauty

I give you myself,
my sleepless nights,
the long draughts
of sky and stars – drunk
upon the mountains,
the breeze of the seas crossed
toward remote dawns.

I give you myself,
the virgin sun of my mornings
on fabulous shores
amid surviving columns
and olives and wheat.

I give you myself,
the noons
on the edge of waterfalls,
the sunsets
at the feet of statues, on the hills,
among trunks of cypresses alive
with nests –

And you receive my wonder
as a creature,
my trembling like a stem
alive in the circle
of horizons,
bent to the clear
wind – of beauty:
and you let me look into these eyes

that God has given you,
so dense with sky –
deep as centuries of light
sunk beyond
the peaks –

4 December 1934

Riconciliazione

La luna è vitrea e lieve
ancora, nel vasto tramonto.
Perché non uscire
di qui? Perché non portare
laggiù, nelle strade, la mia
nostalgia dei monti perduti,
tradurla in amore
pel mondo
che amai?

Già troppo soffersero
del mio rancore
le cose: e vivere non si può
a lungo
se silenziosamente piangono
le cose, su noi.

Stasera, stasera,
quando i volti degli uomini
saran macchie d'ombra e non più –
quando le case
al sommo
sole vivranno di luce –
io troverò me stessa
nel vecchio mondo
e profondo
sarà l'abbraccio
delle cose con me.

Riconteremo i fili

che legano i miei occhi
agli occhi illuminati delle vie,
riconteremo i passi
per cui l'anima versa
la sua sete di strade
sopra la buia terra –

Forse le cose
perdoneranno ancora –
forse, facendo
delle gran braccia arco
su me,
pergolati di sogni stenderanno
domani sovra il mio
solitario meriggio.

3 novembre 1933

Reconciliation

The moon is glassy and light
still, in the vast sunset.
Why not go
out from here? Why not carry
down there, into the streets, my
nostalgia for the lost mountains,
turn it into love
for the world
I loved?

Too long have the things
suffered
from my resentment: and one cannot live
long
if silently the things
weep
over us.

Tonight, tonight,
when the faces of men
will be patches of shadow and no more –
when the houses
at the crest
will live in the sun's light –
I shall find myself
in the old world
and deep
will be the embrace
of things with me.

We shall recount the threads
that tie my eyes
to the street-lit eyes of the ways,
we shall recount the steps
by which the soul pours out
its thirst for roads
upon the dark earth –

Perhaps the things
will forgive once more –
perhaps, making
their great arms into an arch
over me,
trellises of dreams they will stretch
tomorrow over my
solitary noon.

3 November 1933

All'amato

Tu sei tornato in me
come la voce
d'uno che giunge,
ch'empie a un tratto la stanza,
quando è già sera.

Qui c'era
soltanto il peso
delle ore irrigidite
in grigiore di pietra,
il passo lento
dei fossati in pianura
sotto nudi archi di pioppi. C'erano
al termine delle case
le povere strade
di novembre, straziate di solchi…

E c'era questo mio vivere
che ripete ogni giorno
il gesto di una mano di carne
calata giù nel profondo
a chiudere la bocca di Dio.
C'era la sabbia
che giù si rovescia
sull'incendio di Dio.
C'era la falce
che morde
le erbe di Dio.
La pietra
che cade sui cani,

sugli uccelli di Dio.
Allora sei tornato
tu – in me –
come la voce
d'uno che giunge,
che nessuno più attende
perché è già sera.

Sei ritornato in me
come un fedele
stormo di rondini
che riappendon nidi
al tetto oscuro del cuore.
Sei ritornato come uno sciame
d'api che cercano
i loro fiori – e indorano
l'orto nativo.

Ora nell'orto io sento
crescere i nuovi
miei fiori per te. Sento spuntare
sui pascoli, dove
la neve si è sciolta,
gli anemoni gialli
e dal suolo del cielo
le stelle – che a quelli somigliano –
le stelle – dopo che il gelo
del vespro è scomparso

6 novembre 1933

To my loved one

You have returned in me
like the voice
of someone arriving,
suddenly filling the room,
when it is already evening.

Here there was
only the weight
of hours stiffened
in a stony greyness,
the slow step
of the ditches in the plain
under naked arches of poplars. There were
at the end of the houses
the poor November
roads, torn with furrows…

And there was this living of mine
that repeats each day
the gesture of a hand of flesh
lowered down into the depths
to close the mouth of God.
There was the sand
falling down
upon the blaze of God.
There was the scythe
that bites
the grasses of God.
The stone
that falls upon dogs,

upon God's birds.
Then you returned
you – in me –
like the voice
of someone arriving
whom no one awaits anymore
for it is already evening.

You returned in me
like a faithful
flock of swallows
that rehang their nests
on the dark roof of the heart.
You returned like a swarm
of bees searching
for their flowers – and gilding
the native garden.

Now in the garden I feel
my new
flowers growing for you. I feel them sprout
on the pastures where
the snow has melted,
the yellow anemones
and from the soil of the sky
the stars – that resemble them –
the stars – after the frost
of dusk has vanished.

6 novembre 1933

Desiderio di cose leggere

Giuncheto lieve biondo
come un campo di spighe
presso il lago celeste
e le case di un'isola lontana
color di vela
pronte a salpare –

Desiderio di cose leggere
nel cuore che pesa
come pietra
dentro una barca –

Ma giungerà una sera
a queste rive
l'anima liberata:
senza piegare i giunchi
senza muovere l'acqua o l'aria
salperà – con le case
dell'isola lontana,
per un'alta scogliera
di stelle –

1 febbraio 1934

Desire for light things

Light blond reeds,
like a field of wheat
by the celestial lake,
and the houses of a distant island,
the colour of sails,
ready to set out—

Desire for light things
in a heart that weighs
like stone
inside a boat—

But one evening
to these shores
the liberated soul will arrive:
without bending the reeds,
without stirring water or air,
it will set sail – with the houses
of the distant island,
toward a high cliff
of stars –

1 February 1934

Preghiera alla poesia

Oh, tu bene mi pesi
l'anima, poesia:
tu sai se io manco e mi perdo,
tu che allora ti neghi
e taci.

Poesia, mi confesso con te
che sei la mia voce profonda:
tu lo sai,
tu lo sai che ho tradito,
ho camminato sul prato d'oro
che fu mio cuore,
ho rotto l'erba,
rovinata la terra –
poesia – quella terra
dove tu mi dicesti il più dolce
di tutti i tuoi canti,
dove un mattino per la prima volta
vidi volar nel sereno l'allodola
e con gli occhi cercai di salire –
Poesia, poesia che rimani
il mio profondo rimorso,
oh aiutami tu a ritrovare
il mio alto paese abbandonato –
Poesia che ti doni soltanto
a chi con occhi di pianto
si cerca –
oh rifammi tu degna di te,
poesia che mi guardi.

Pasturo, 23 agosto 1934

Prayer to poetry

Oh, you weigh upon me
my soul, poetry:
you know when I fail and lose myself,
you who then withdraw
and fall silent.

Poetry, I confess to you
who are my deepest voice:
you know,
you know that I have betrayed,
I have walked on the golden meadow
that was my heart,
I have broken the grass,
ruined the earth –
poetry – that earth
where you told me the sweetest
of all your songs,
where one morning for the first time
I saw the lark fly in the clear sky
and with my eyes tried to rise –
Poetry, poetry who remain
my profound remorse,
oh help me find again
my high abandoned homeland –
Poetry who give yourself only
to those who with tearful eyes
search themselves –
oh remake me worthy of you,
poetry who look upon me.

Pasturo, 23 August 1934

Lieve offerta

Vorrei che la mia anima ti fosse
leggera
come le estreme foglie
dei pioppi, che s'accendono di sole
in cima ai tronchi fasciati
di nebbia –

Vorrei condurti con le mie parole
per un deserto viale, segnato
d'esili ombre –
fino a una valle d'erboso silenzio,
al lago –
ove tinnisce per un fiato d'aria
il canneto
e le libellule si trastullano
con l'acqua non profonda –

Vorrei che la mia anima ti fosse
leggera,
che la mia poesia ti fosse un ponte,
sottile e saldo,
bianco –
sulle oscure voragini
della terra.

5 dicembre 1934

Light offer

I wish that my soul were
light for you
like the last leaves
of the poplars, flaring with sun
at the top of trunks
bandaged with mist –

I wish to lead you with my words
through a deserted avenue, traced
with slender shadows –
down to a valley of grassy silence,
to the lake –
where for a breath of air
the reeds tinkle
and the dragonflies play
with the shallow water –

I wish that my soul were
light for you,
that my poetry were for you a bridge,
thin and firm,
white –
over the dark chasms
of the earth.

5 December 1934

Incantesimi

Alti orli ghiacciati
si disfecero al mondo.
Solcava
lenta e lieve la barca
laghi d'oro,
andando così noi nel sole
abbracciati.
Gracili reti bionde
imprigionavano l'ora.
E nacquero brividi;
crebbero
voci tristi;
fischiò
a sponda il dilacerarsi delle canne.
Belve chiare
guardarono dal folto
a lungo
il tramonto nell'acqua,
andando così verso l'ombra
io libera
e sola per sempre.

22 dicembre 1935

Enchantments

Tall icy rims
came undone into the world.
Slow and light
the boat furrowed
lakes of gold,
and so we went on in the sun,
embraced.
Slender blond nets
imprisoned the hour.
And shivers were born;
there grew
sad voices;
along the bank
the rending of the reeds whistled.
Pale beasts
watched from the thicket,
for a long time,
the sunset in the water,
and so I went toward the shadow,
free,
and alone forever.

22 December 1935

Messaggio

E tu, stella acuta notturna
splendi ancora
se per il solco delle strade
grida la triste anima dei cani.
Sorgeranno colline d'erba magra
a coprirti:
ma nel mio buio conquistato
brillerai, fuoco bianco,
parlando ai vivi della mia morte.

21–22 giugno 1937

Message

And you, sharp nocturnal star,
you shine still
if along the furrow of the roads
the sad soul of dogs cries out.
Hills of thin grass
will rise to cover you:
but in my conquered darkness
you will shine, white fire,
speaking to the living of my death.

21–22 June 1937

Pudore

Se qualcuna delle mie povere parole
ti piace
e tu me lo dici
sia pur solo con gli occhi
io mi spalanco
in un riso beato
ma tremo
come una mamma piccola giovane
che perfino arrossisce
se un passante le dice
che il suo bambino è bello.

1 febbraio 1933

Modesty

If one of my humble words
pleases you
and you tell me so,
even only with your eyes,
I open wide
into a blessed smile
but I tremble,
like a small young mother
who blushes even
when passerby tells her
that her child is beautiful.

1 February 1933

Notturno

Curva tu suoni
ed il tuo canto è un albero d'argento
nel silenzio oscuro –
Limpido nasce
dal tuo labbro – il profilo
delle vette – nel buio –
Muoiono le tue note
come gocce assorbite dalla terra –
Le nebbie sopra gli abissi
percorse dal vento
sollevano il suono spento
nel cielo –

(Breil, luglio 1933 – Pasturo, 22 agosto 1933)

Nocturne

Bent, you play,
and your song is a silver tree
in the dark silence –
Clear it is born
from your lips – the outline
of peaks – in the night –
Your notes die
like drops absorbed by the earth –
Mists above the abysses,
traversed by the wind,
lift the extinguished sound
into the sky –

(Breil, July 1933 – Pasturo, 22 August 1933)

Saresti stato

Annunzio
saresti stato
di quel che non fummo,
di quello che fummo
e che non siamo più.
In te sarebbero
ritornati i morti
e vissuti i non nati,
sgorgate le acque
sepolte.
La poesia,
da noi amata e non sciolta
dal cuore mai,
tu l'avresti cantata
con gridi di fanciullo.
L'unica spiga
di due zolle confuse
eri tu –
lo stelo
della nostra innocenza
sotto il sole.
Ma sei rimasto laggiù,
con i morti,
con i non nati,
con le acque
sepolte –
alba già spenta al lume
delle ultime stelle:
non occupa ora terra
ma solo

cuore
la tua invisibile
bara.

22 ottobre 1933

You would have been

A herald
you would have been
of what we were not,
of what we were
and are no longer.
In you
the dead would have returned
and the unborn lived,
the buried waters
would have sprung forth.
Poetry,
loved by us and never loosened
from the heart,
you would have sung
with a child's cries.
The single ear of wheat
from two confused clods
you were –
the stem
of our innocence
under the sun.
But you remained down there,
with the dead,
with the unborn,
with the buried
waters –
a dawn already extinguished in the glow
of the last stars:
now it occupies no ground
but only

the heart,
your invisible
coffin.

22 October 1933

Tre sere

La prima sera ci fu la pioggia
nera assordante –
ed io al crocicchio,
a decifrare nomi
di strade sconosciute –
sola alle soglie
di una città nuova,
sola con la mia preda
di felicità – con l'eco
della tua voce.

Poi, sopra i monti, fu la limpidezza
bruciante della notte –
e sulla neve riflesse
le innumeri stelle
ed adagiate nell'argenteo sonno
l'esili ombre
dei rami –
Io sola, io limpida tutta,
nel vento lieve di settentrione,
io in pace
con la chiarezza del cielo,
con il diffuso ricordo
del tuo sguardo.

Stasera la nebbia, candore sordo,
intorno al tremito della mia
attesa – velo
sulla parola non detta,
difesa – per la paura del tempo,

per la fretta
di vivere.
Pausa – Di nebbia s'avvolge
il cuore
colmo e sospeso,
per non udire
i suoi battiti.

1° dicembre 1934

Three evenings

The first evening there was rain,
black, deafening –
and I at the crossroads,
deciphering names
of unfamiliar streets –
alone on the threshold
of a new city,
alone with my quarry
of happiness – with the echo
of your voice.

Then, above the mountains, came the searing
clarity of night –
and on the snow were mirrored
the countless stars,
and laid to rest in silvery sleep
the slender shadows
of branches –
I alone, wholly clear,
in the light northern wind,
at peace
with the brightness of the sky,
with the diffused memory
of your gaze.

Tonight the fog, a muffled whiteness,
around the tremor of my
waiting – a veil
over the unspoken word,
a defense – against the fear of time,

against the haste
to live.
Pause —In fog the heart wraps itself,
full and suspended,
so as not to hear
its own beating.

1 December 1934

Secondo amore

Piansi bambina, per un mondo
più grande del mio cuore,
dentro il mio cuore
rinchiuso – morto;
piansi con occhi giovani,
penosamente arsi arrosati –
e sola vicina alla terra
domandavo agli oggetti muti,
alle radici dei fiori divelti,
alle ali degli insetti caduti,
il perché
del morire.

Mi rispondeva la terra, fedele,
prima ancora che fosse
primavera colma,
da anni e secoli – sotto un arbusto
con una pallida primula
rifiorita.
E in essa era la linfa,
era il respiro – di tutte
le primavere perdute,
in ogni fiore vivo la bellezza
degli innumeri fiori
spenti.

Oh grazia – ora dico –
del secondo amore,
giovinezza profonda intessuta
di vinte vecchiezze, di esistenze percorse –

– ed ogni esistenza, una ricchezza
conquisa, ogni pianto deterso
un sorriso più lungo imparato,
ogni percossa, una carezza più lieve
che si vorrebbe donare –
oh benedetto il mio pianto
– ora dico –
benedetti i miei occhi
di bimba, arrossati riarsi –
benedetto il soffrire, il morire
di tutti i mondi che portai nel cuore –
se dalla morte si rinasce
un giorno,
se dalla morte io rinasco
oggi – per te,
me stessa offrendo
alle tue mani – come
una corolla
di dissepolte vite.

4 dicembre 1934

Second love

I wept as a child, for a world
larger than my heart,
within my heart
sealed – dead;
I wept with young eyes,
painfully scorched and reddened –
and alone, close to the earth,
I asked mute objects,
the roots of uprooted flowers,
the wings of fallen insects,
the reason
for dying.

The earth answered me, faithful,
even before it became
full spring,
for years and centuries – beneath a shrub
with a pale primrose
flowering again.
And in it was the sap,
the breath – of all
lost springs,
in every living flower the beauty
of the countless flowers
extinguished.

Oh grace – I say now –
of the second love,
a deep youth woven
with conquered old ages, with lives traversed –

– and every life, a richness
won, every tear wiped away
a longer smile learned,
every blow a gentler caress
one longs to give –
Oh blessed be my weeping –
I say now –
blessed be my eyes,
as a child, reddened, scorched –
blessed be the suffering, the dying
of all the worlds I carried in my heart –
if from death one is reborn
one day,
if from death I am reborn
today – for you,
offering myself,
to your hands – like
a corolla
of lives lifted from burial.

4 December 1934

Lieve offerta

Vorrei che la mia anima ti fosse
leggera
come le estreme foglie
dei pioppi, che s'accendono di sole
in cima ai tronchi fasciati
di nebbia –

Vorrei condurti con le mie parole
per un deserto viale, segnato
d'esili ombre –
fino a una valle d'erboso silenzio,
al lago –
ove tinnisce per un fiato d'aria
il canneto
e le libellule si trastullano
con l'acqua non profonda –

Vorrei che la mia anima ti fosse
leggera,
che la mia poesia ti fosse un ponte,
sottile e saldo,
bianco –
sulle oscure voragini
della terra.

5 dicembre 1934

Light offering

I wish my soul to be
light for you,
like the highest leaves
of the poplars, kindled by the sun
at the tops of trunks wrapped
in mist –

I wish to lead you with my words
along a deserted avenue, marked
by slender shadows –
to a valley of grassy silence,
to the lake –
where, at a breath of air,
the reed bed chimes
and dragonflies amuse themselves
with the shallow water –

I wish my soul might be
light for you,
that my poetry might be a bridge for you,
slender and sure,
white –
over the dark abysses
of the earth.

5 December 1934

Pausa

Mi pareva che questa giornata
senza te
dovesse essere inquieta,
oscura. Invece è colma
di una strana dolcezza, che s'allarga
attraverso le ore –
forse com'è la terra
dopo uno scroscio,
che resta sola nel silenzio a bersi
l'acqua caduta
e a poco a poco
nelle più fonde vene se ne sente
penetrata.

La gioia che ieri fu angoscia,
tempesta –
ora ritorna a brevi
tonfi sul cuore,
come un mare placato:
al mite sole riapparso brillano,
candidi doni,
le conchiglie che l'onda
lasciò sul lido.

7 dicembre 1934

Pause

It seemed to me that this day
without you
should have been restless,
dark. Instead it is full
of a strange sweetness, spreading
through the hours –
perhaps as the earth is
after a downpour,
left alone in silence to drink
the fallen water,
and little by little
to feel it seep
into its deepest veins.

The joy that yesterday was anguish,
Storm –
now returns in brief
throbs upon the heart,
like a calmed sea:
under the gentle sun reappeared,
they gleam, like candid gifts,
the shells the wave
left upon the shore.

7 December 1934

Confidare

Ho tanta fede in te. Mi sembra
che saprei aspettare la tua voce
in silenzio, per secoli
di oscurità.

Tu sai tutti i segreti,
come il sole:
potresti far fiorire
i gerani e la zàgara selvaggia
sul fondo delle cave
di pietra, delle prigioni
leggendarie.

Ho tanta fede in te. Son quieta
come l'arabo avvolto
nel barracano bianco,
che ascolta Dio maturargli
l'orzo intorno alla casa.

8 dicembre 1934

To trust

I have such faith in you. It seems to me
I could wait for your voice
in silence, for centuries
of darkness.

You know every secret,
like the sun:
you could make geraniums bloom
and wild orange blossom
at the bottom of stone quarries,
of legendary
prisons.

I have such faith in you. I am calm
like the Arab wrapped
in his white burnous,
who listens to God ripen
the barley around his house.

8 December 1934

L'àncora

Sono rimasta sola nella notte:
ho sul volto il sapore del tuo pianto,
intorno alla persona
il silenzio – che sul tonfo
della porta richiusa, a larghi cerchi
si riappiana.

Lenta nell'acqua oscura
del cuore –
lenta e sicura,
tra le alghe profonde
gli echi delle tempeste le lunghe correnti
le molli ghirlande di onde
intorno a inabissati
scogli –

lenta e sicura,
fino alle sabbie segrete giacenti
sul fondo dell'essere –
fida tenace, con i suoi tre bracci
lucenti
penetra l'àncora
delle tue tre parole:
– Tu aspetta me –.

16 dicembre 1934

The anchor

I have remained alone in the night:
upon my face the taste of your tears,
around my body
the silence – which, from the thud
of the door shut again, in wide circles
smooths itself flat.

Slow in the dark water
of the heart –
slow and sure,
among deep seaweed,
the echoes of storms, the long currents,
the yielding garlands of waves
around sunken
reefs –

slow and sure,
down to the secret sands lying
at the bottom of my being –
faithful, tenacious, with its three shining
arms
the anchor of your three words
pierces me:
– Wait for me –

16 December 1934

Sgorgo

Per troppa vita che ho nel sangue
tremo
nel vasto inverno.

E all'improvviso,
come per una fonte che si scioglie
nella steppa,
una ferita che nel sonno
si riapre,

perdutamente nascono pensieri
nel deserto castello della notte.

Creatura di fiaba, per le mute
stanze, dove si struggono le lampade
dimenticate,
lieve trascorre una parola bianca:
si levano colombe sull'altana
come alla vista del mare.

Bontà, tu mi ritorni:
si stempera l'inverno nello sgorgo
del mio più puro sangue,
ancora il pianto ha dolcemente nome
perdono.

12 gennaio 1935

Springing forth

For too much life I carry in my blood
I tremble
in the vast winter.

And all at once,
as when a spring wells out
in the dry plains,
a wound that in sleep
reopens,

thoughts are born hopelessly
in the desert castle of the night.

A fairytale creature, through the mute
rooms where forgotten lamps
waste away,
a white, weightless word passes:
doves rise on the terrace
as at the sight of the sea.

Goodness, you return to me:
winter thins and melts in the springing forth
of my purest blood,
once more even weeping bears, gently, the name
of forgiveness.

12 January 1935

Atene

Con l'alba
dal mare salivo
per alte scalee: si piegavano
cieli d'attesa ai margini
della pietra.

E traboccò per la spianata il sole.
Tepidi fiotti corsero nei fusti
delle colonne,
dense vene si aprirono
di linfa bionda:

si levarono i templi nella luce
come mani vive

e misuravo tra le aeree dita
gli spazi
di un eterno mattino.

(20 aprile 1934) 28 gennaio 1935

Athens

At dawn
from the sea I climbed
on high stairways: while there were bending
skies of expectancy along the edges
of stone.

And the sun overflowed across the esplanade.
Warm currents ran through the shafts
of the columns,
dense veins opened
with golden sap:

the temples rose into the light
like living hands,

and I measured, between their airy fingers,
the spaces
of an eternal morning.

(20 April 1934) 28 January 1935

Il sentiero

Sperare
mentre il domani intatto sconfina
e tosto
dimenticare il volto
delle speranze, nel tempo vero.

Viali sognavi per la vita
e un esile
sentiero ti rimane.

Una sera
la tua montagna si ricorderà
di averti avuta
bambina
sul suo grembo d'erba;
e lontana vedendoti
a cercare
su perse rive le ombre
delle tue cose sepolte,
ti chiamerà coi cenni
antichi – delle campane.

Il tuo sentiero ti ricondurrà
lungo la valle,
per la conca prativa – al muro candido,
al cancello socchiuso.

Lassù, nel breve orto disteso
ai ritorni delle stagioni, ai cieli
della neve e dei venti

primaverili,
verranno bocche
di bambini sconosciuti
a cantare
sulla tua solitudine.

30 gennaio 1935

The path

To hope
while the untouched tomorrow spills over,
and swiftly
to forget the face
of hopes, in true time.

You dreamed of avenues for your life,
and a slender
path remains to you.

One evening
your mountain will remember
having held you
as a child
on its grassy lap;
and seeing you far away,
seeking
on lost shores the shadows
of your buried things,
it will call you with the ancient
nods – of the bells.

Your path will lead you back
down the valley,
through the meadowed hollow – to the white wall,
to the half–open gate.

Up there, in the small garden laid open
to the returns of the seasons, to the skies
of snow and of spring

winds,
mouths of unknown children
will come to sing
of your solitude.

30 January 1935

L'ava

T'abbraccio per sentire la tua carne
pregna di pace e vicina a morire –
fresca e tetra così
presso il mio fiato.
Di là dalle parole: ed ascoltiamo
al polso uguali battiti – ed un solo
ultimo abbeverarsi della vita.
A riva di neri laghi
torna a prender luce
quest'occhio da te sola fatto azzurro;
così prendendomi al tuo grembo
e chiusa nel tuo alvo
profondo, una divengo
al tuo peso mortale che vanisce:
tanto che non ci stacchi più la terra –
ma ad entrambe si faccia buia e lieve.

1° maggio 1937

The ancestor[2]

I hold you to feel your flesh,
laden with peace and close to dying –
fresh and somber so,
near my breath.
Beyond words: and we listen
at the wrist to equal pulses – and one single,
final draught of life.
On the shore of black lakes
this eye, made blue by you alone,
returns to take in light;
and so, taking me to your breast
and enclosed within your deep
womb, I become one
with your mortal weight as it fades:
so much so that the earth no longer parts us –
but grows dark and gentle for us both.

1 May 1937

---

[2] *"Ava"* in Italian means a female ancestor, a grandmother or great grandmother. This poem is dedicated to Pozzi's grandmother Nena.

Poetry collections by Stefania Lucchetti

Italian Poetry in Translation

GIFT GUIDE

Book	Perfect gift for
Coffee Stains on My Books **Penelope's Web**	Friend, mother, sister, wife, adult daughter
Love Poems	Anyone you love
Afternoons of Suspended Love	Your wife, husband, a friend who has been married for a long time
Poetry is Cyberpunk **Digital Citizenship**	The intellectual reader looking for a reflective book
Italian Women Poets collection	The reader interested in world poetry in translation

Essays by Stefania Lucchetti

Printed in Dunstable, United Kingdom

84577022R00077